ARBOROPHOBIA

NANCY HOLMES

ARBOROPHOBIA

UNIVERSITY *of* **ALBERTA** PRESS

Published by

University of Alberta Press
1–16 Rutherford Library South
11204 89 Avenue NW
Edmonton, Alberta, Canada T6G 2J4
Amiskwacîwâskahican | Treaty 6 |
Métis Territory
uap.ualberta.ca

Copyright © 2022 Nancy Holmes

LIBRARY AND ARCHIVES CANADA
CATALOGUING IN PUBLICATION

Title: Arborophobia / Nancy Holmes.
Names: Holmes, Nancy, 1959– author.
Series: Robert Kroetsch series.
Description: Series statement: Robert Kroetsch
    series | Poems.
Identifiers: Canadiana (print) 20210373083 |
    Canadiana (ebook) 20210373105 |
    ISBN 9781772126020 (softcover) |
    ISBN 9781772126105 (EPUB) |
    ISBN 9781772126112 (PDF)
Classification: LCC PS8565.O637 A73 2022 |
    DDC C811/.54—dc23

First edition, first printing, 2022.
First printed and bound in Canada by
Houghton Boston Printers, Saskatoon,
Saskatchewan.
Copyediting by Sharon Thesen.
Proofreading by Mary Lou Roy.

A volume in the Robert Kroetsch Series.

All rights reserved. No part of this publication
may be produced, stored in a retrieval system,
or transmitted in any form or by any means
(electronic, mechanical, photocopying,
recording, or otherwise) without prior written
consent. Contact University of Alberta Press
for further details.

University of Alberta Press supports copyright.
Copyright fuels creativity, encourages diverse
voices, promotes free speech, and creates a
vibrant culture. Thank you for buying an
authorized edition of this book and for complying
with the copyright laws by not reproducing,
scanning, or distributing any part of it in any
form without permission. You are supporting
writers and allowing University of Alberta
Press to continue to publish books for
every reader.

University of Alberta Press is committed to
protecting our natural environment. As part
of our efforts, this book is printed on Enviro
Paper: it contains 100% post-consumer
recycled fibres and is acid- and chlorine-free.

University of Alberta Press gratefully
acknowledges the support received for its
publishing program from the Government of
Canada, the Canada Council for the Arts, and
the Government of Alberta through the Alberta
Media Fund.

Canada   Canada Council   Conseil des Arts
                for the Arts   du Canada
Alberta
Government

for Sue Palmer
in gratitude for decades of loving friendship
and in memory of Lori Mairs
who talked with the trees

He showed a little thing the quantity of a hazelnut in the palm of my hand, and it was as round as a ball. I looked thereupon with the eye of my understanding and thought, "What may this be?" And it was answered thus, "It is all that is made."

—JULIAN OF NORWICH

CONTENTS

V PATH

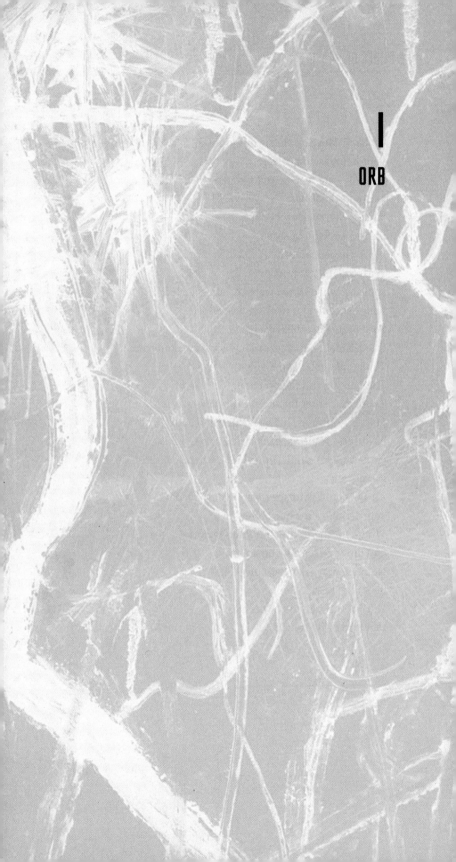

ORB

Give me your spikelets, your glumes,
your lemmas and paleas.
Give me your sedges and fescues,
oats and timothies.
Such awns, such ascending,
barbed, beaked, bearded,
heart-shaped, bladed.
With collars and bristles,
some crowned, some webbed, some keeled.
Songs succulent, tawny, and sheathed.
Seeds canoed, seeds like pears.
Dances incurved, dances long, swaying, and pale.
Those palatable. Those silky.
The humble and the nodding.
Those that enter the mouths of the grazers.
Marshes, prairies, hillsides, alpine, woods,
pastures, meadows, backyards, parks, fields,
gardens, wastelands, gravel pits, wrecks, deserts, sand:
all yours.
All subject to your spears and your invaders,
your strings and your orchestras.
Where do you not scatter your gestures
and fling your grainy notes?
No savannah exists without you,
no loaf of bread.
You are the feathers of the earth,
that bird of the sun.

THE MILK CHUTE, AN ODE

i.

double-doored chamber
into white stucco house

ear with rattling glass bones

barnacle
with children's fingers in it

jewel box for green glass and pebbles
"drink me" paper lids

the milkman's hands
in the wall of our house

obsolete hole boarded up
beneath a renovation

ii.

when I was sixty my mother
        gave me her pearls
                my father's wedding gift

for decades
        a black velvet sachet
                polished their slinky weight

I remember white drops
        of milk
                beading around my nipples

I remember
  a baby's tooth stretching
    shiny gums

  a shell
    razoring through

  then a necklace of teeth
    erupting

iii.

to this day I cannot find
the exact milk chute shade
to paint my kitchen

not Mascarpone nor Cloud Nine
not Egyptian Flax nor Palomino

to this day I look for an opening
into that house

but with a coat of crushed stone
and drywall
the threshold is sealed

iv.

pearls descend
  from the maternal line

doors slide open
then click
  shut

eggs and milky sperm roll over
    each other

empty bottles rinsed

    a standstill in the portal

        each day a hinge of time

coldest snowy days of winter
when dawn is purple

bluest summer mornings
    when clouds blow out
        and clouds cave in

SPRING SHAVE

that barber Winter
with its clippers
Ice and Storm
hacks down straw, chaff
all that's messy, seedy, stiff and stalky
anything brittle, tall, dry
sticking up above the snow

but there's no keeping that buzz cut
when the slopping lather
of April comes

everything grows out of control
even with a daily
trim and shave

water birds duck low

thick migrations clog the razors

rashes of seedlings bend unharmed
beneath the blade

while springy branches
bounce right up unscathed

and the robin

misses decapitation
just in time
as it bows down
to honour
the elastic worm

LUNOLIO

dear erratic pendulum moon
it is only you thou you that I so address
o moon moon
lap lap lapping up that track on the lake
the baying all night
moon o moon

canoe-hipped boygirl
mountain tongs
grasping the cartwheeling clavicle, you
gob of spit
larva pearl
cell of galactic
honeycomb you

wading up to knee wrist belly
skin parting for you to thee
slender-ankled queenking
teeth beaming, bones opening tubes to
moon marrow
moon pin at dawn, moon needle at night
o moon dear moon
dear pendulum pots and pans banging moon

head banger, eye rolling
unspeakable moon
you're not going anywhere
you're on your leash
you're barking up the wrong sea
you're howling, baring your fangs

foaming spittle all over the sky
those nip pricking
puppy teeth
worried my finger
but now I ignore your
pock-face leer
most of the time

      most of the lecherous time
big winker
there's no getting away from your paws
you reach round
mound and house
spy through windows with ultrasound eyes
      well, I keep that moon-coloured scar
out for you
but hang my body
in a dark closet
on my chicken bones

      on my swinging, swaying body
you marked me from birth
moon stamped on fingernails
new moon breasts, moon wax
      layered in buttock and thigh
puckered womb glove
once full of moon babies
with rows of snacking teeth
and translucent spines
and so many more eggs falling out
fallopian tubes
      into the fringy night

       fringe, furbelow, sashay and bewilder
moon o moon
dear ecstatic
cross-dressing moon
thy radiant underwear on the floor
       moon o moon
blade, tentacle, chain
you cratered and cupped me
my carpenter and my aquarium
       your exquisite sloshing
       your monthly
hammer hammer hammer

have you really stopped jerking me around?
       we smile, we bow
I hobble after you
you bring a ceremony
on a platter, an iced cake
we eyeball each other
we drink tea from cups with saucers
one day I shall step into thy boat
my feet like wafers
breaking
       dazzling moon, dear terrifying hit-by-a-tide
       moon

ANEMONE IN CYPRUS

> I find objects and they give me their ideas.
> —HORST WEIERSTALL

This is the flower of the anemone.
In moonlight it is baked
into microscope.
The eye in the microscope looks up at you.
Is that an eyelash or is the glass cracked?

This is the flower of the anemone.
A small wheel with delicate spokes.
The bruise of love where the wheel runs over you.
A button on the kid glove of earth.
The buttons and collars
that make you fumble.
The pulse in the throat.

This is the flower of the anemone.
The hole between earth and air.
This is a hole.
A bullet hole
petalling through flesh.
The flower of the anemone adds feathers to
the shifting shadows of clouds in the grass.

This is the flower of the anemone.
A navel that changes the slope of the belly,
puckered
like a newborn's fist.
A peel, a paring,
a strip of the inner thigh
of gored Adonis.

The flower of the anemone is one stitch
making a hole in the veil.
The flower of the anemone is because the stitch
both sinks and rises
through a net of holes,
through grasses,
through skin.
The flower of the anemone turns clothing inside out
so threads and eyelashes
dangle from their holes
like cliff swallows
slipping in and out.
With our collars, we
are sprung open.

The flower of the anemone is an earlobe.
A testicle.
A bubble in the throat.
A metal sliver in your thumb.
A dish for your elbow.
An insect's stinger
and a kiss.

The flower of the anemone is an eyelash against a boulder.
The eyelash entices you, drops
the boulder on you.
This is the bait that draws you
into the dirt, into the hole,
a hole made with your finger,
a hole in the eye surrounded by purple iris,
the hole where the eye of earth looks up.

SAINT LUCY

(who carries her eyes in a dish)

May I offer you an eye?
A young woman's orb
freshly plucked.
The lens a clear lozenge
not yellowed with age.
Inside, a layer
of chocolatey retina
and a filling of gel,
not even a lump
or a floater.
A ball uncataracted,
cleansed of lid and lash.
Its blue iris
anise-flavoured,
I speculate,
to accompany the gush
of ocular salt
on the tongue.

NEWBORN

before the baby begins to smile
it lives in a caustic state
its black eyes and open mouth
small explosions
as the world ignites the body
with oxygen
and a milky acid snake
twists from throat to anus

fallen from the cosmic rope
its hands recoil then catch the burning air
its budding organs are skewered
to the harsh world

it cannot help but
make its terrible noises

star dropped in a bucket of lime
glossy nut cut by the soil's sore teeth
small soul spat out

when the smile comes
there's no turning back
blistered and scorched
the lips mouth *I'm here*
splinters on the windowsill
notwithstanding
diving head first
onto this barbed and
scalding planet—

II

ARBOROPHOBIA

PONDEROSA PINE

I. GOTCHA

pines riding their roots
hot-rodding

green *kapows*
scattering the birds

pines blitzed, strutting
sometimes hassling a risky nest

though I fear
there's precious little
egg-laying going on

not in that
wooden kimono
not under that
cracking whip

this vandal
wrecked the fence
crashed right down into my yard

I knew those hoods partied
night and day

bunch of juvies on the hill
tagging the slopes
littering the paths
with their needles

but this
insult, this
eff you

this flip-off
pine quiff

I'm calling the cops,
the bylaw guys, the tree feller—
whoever, whatever
you're toast

we're going
to hell in a handcart
plants riot over
every inch
of seawater and soil
Plankton
or Pine—
who gets the biggest chunk of my taxes?
roots and slime
getting wasted
cashing their cheques
chucking their
green trash
and needles
everywhere
feckless spongers
flogging the waves
whining for the moon

I took it into my home
a foster child
a freshly fallen pine cone
scales smooth and sweet
as a baby's knuckles

you can say *told ya*
but still it shocks me
that when the heat's on
the ungrateful little bastard
bares its claws

made-to-murder pine
multi-fisted
comb-tracks in your hair
tossing your locks
with the talons of a hawk
zippers of your hoodie wide open
all those chainsaw teeth

you're slingshot, handcuffed to
wind
hanging off parched hillside
like a thug on a bus
going nowhere
going nowhere fast
big buddy

yes
some of you ponder
some bristle
but about what?
all those subsidies, all the do-gooders
protesting on the hill
always after something
your roots crawl into the cracks
your bark bursts the bank
admit it:
you think you're better
than everyone else
you and your great whacking limbs
just itching
to break down the house

you're toast now baby
      after the fire
your trunk split open
and we found your
stash of weapons

a chopper squad jumped out
and *shing, shing, shing*
all those orange
flick knives
      sprang up

we mowed you down

gotcha

always sassing
always giving us grief
your bark and snarls
and big bad brute force
lurking beneath those branches

but watch your cocky swagger
old sticks
we're going to level
that playing field
yes, we, your biggest nightmare
the hatchet men

II. QUALMS

I have had others before the pine in my heart.
I have bowed down before drawings of many a deciduous tree.
I have taken the name of *Pinus ponderosa* in vain,
both in English and in Latin.
I have not remembered the day of the pine and kept it holy.
I have not honoured the pine cone, the fire, the aquifer,
and the squirrel for many of the years I have lived on this earth.
In the casket of my house are a pine bowl, a pine shelf,
and a pine floor, as well as some ashes.
I have committed unspeakable black-and-white betrayals
beneath the pine's kaleidoscopic eye.
I have been permissive on the needle-carpeted paths.
I have wanted it all, all the inside-out wooden wealth
of the pine.
In penance I kneel before the pine's leather jacket
and wait for the cougar to fall upon my neck.

if I say
you are the furnishing of my tabernacle
with your oiled light
your purple and scarlet linen, oxblood leather
ram's skin dyed red, bristling badger skin
your orchid incense

if I worship your glowing crown
your hundred celestial rings

may I sit in your branches
in the mercy seat
rocked by cherubim of sun and rain?

may I tarry and abide
in the music
of your bark
all shingled
with tambourine bells?

you're on the catwalk
birds on your branchy fingers
smoke twirled into your hair
morning sunshine silver on your wrists
you dab a drop of that vanilla perfume
and shimmy up the rocky ladder
you ignore that bit of beetle acne
and birds opening their
annoying beaks
to cat-call, no not *cat*
call, I promise I
won't mention *cat* again
because I know that although the twitter
cramps your style
you want those birds anyway
their wings so accessorize
your sashay

you gorgeous tassel

you torch in taffeta
green swing dress

wind ballrooms
your skirt
into whooshing bell

lanterns your long leg
that enflames

goes up
in flames

when I was a child
a comb could pull a shriek out of me
I was full of sensitivities and
qualms

now the wind runs through me easily
not a snag, not a doubt

I don't know, I don't know how
I got to be so callous
so scornful of ... let's be honest
what's left of our beauty

and what is left?
mutton dressed up as
jab of Botox in the fronds
falsie this and that
hair plausible green and then
embeetled, that deceptive
turn to
henna orange

evermore intervention:
peels, waxes, wraps,
ortho, sculpting, laser and
abrasions

now that time is short
we seek—
and then submit to—
any kind of treatment

oh Christ don't just stand there
do something
get the stretcher
it's emergency room fire season
paws wrapped in gauzy air
foot bandaged in felted earth
burning up, falling, broken hips

look at you making a scene up there
if you do have a message for us
eat it,
there's no time for it
no time

        sister crone
even as a sapling you
were as dry and cracked
as an old woman's finger

        sister crone
you may be wise
but also cranky
bitter, suspicious
emotional still
clutching handfuls
of prickling needles
as gift·
as bitching

        sister crone
why can't I imagine
the reach
of your blackening root?

III
STAIN

EARLY SPRING ELEGY

A green blur tangled in winter branches.
Maples braiding both black and nimble limbs.
Could we live so knitted with our dead?
Must they be buried deep or fed to flames?

At dawn, frosted hills are round and rosy
Like strawberries, until daylight moulds them grey.
Over the wrists of trees, daylight drops
The golden shackles, eternal chains of change.

I hide the clock in the basement next to a stone
But spring returns, a beloved, exhausting guest.
An uprooted crocus laid in her coffin makes two
Living wonders gone, ground to ash.

MOTHER JULIAN IMAGINES ONE DROP OF CHRIST'S BLOOD AS THE SCALE OF A HERRING

she spills
a mint of silver sequins
across a reeking deck
a million aromatic gongs
singing from the red mouth of the sea
        God's love
more copious than
the herring's innumerable plenty

but our insolence knows no bounds
nets parachute into the size of islands
        every fish scaled and slammed through a gutter
industries sack the ocean, nations rummage
elbow-deep in wriggling, squirming
bins, boatloads and bargains

it's raining outside the church
bulldozing fish-scales
and blood
        the stone sill
where Julian rests her elbows
is drenched
        she is amazed
that we are loved, restored, hauled
up century after
century despite our endless
selling, killing, torture
and so on and so forth
ad nauseam
she fingers the cool links
of the chain holding the keys
of her cell
angling

big rains coming
big winds zippering open the lake
spitting out crows & making stuff tumble-
weed over
the whole
let's-build-a-subdivision meadow

winds can't take It
down though

It stumbles, It trips, Its
clothes blow up, It
blunders, but— you know this—
       It keeps on
deaf to the hymns
of the symbionts
keeps kicking Its way
out from under the thumb
of the topsoil

It'll teeter, totter, lurch
keep on trying to launch up
right,
& why?
to toil, to lug junk, to bitch
while looking around at the view
there'd be good weather
if we just got rid of
the north & the west
& now that smoky south
It's not even being, It's not confessing—
not to you, not to me, not to no one ever—

It'll just end up
plotting & scheming &
      oops, toe on a root
      and
head over heels   It pitches
Itself   off
the cliff

THE TIME BEING

The "now" is the link of time ...
—ARISTOTLE

i.

I've been distracted by running the world.
I didn't hear the soft snuffling
of the clock.
The earth's dark side meant nothing to me.
A fly buzzing, the sound of skin
shedding, the slow unzipping
of the body from time:
I didn't notice.

ii.

Once, only one family had the time.
With a weekly trip to Greenwich
and a chronometer,
they sold and carried True Time,
their commodity.
It was treasure for trains,
and stock for town clocks.
Now we all get true time for free—
that signal after the long dash is exactly
ten o'clock.
Yet why is it always
Daylight Saving in my car?
Why do so many appointments
hijack my calendar?
And how is it that I don't know
a single family
with any time at all?

iii.

Our cities are experiencing
excessive levels of time.
Too many brown people are having to do time
instead of spending it.
Everyone knows there's a time wave.
The elderly are timing out.
Chronophobia is epidemic.
How long can this crisis last?
Hundreds of thousands of worn-out dates on calendars.
The endless charade of timers on ovens
and infinitely more time needed
to shower and dress.
Why do we keep inviting it to our parties?
Why does it start our parties so late and end them so early?
And those ridiculous birds have theirs
at five in the morning
since they use the big wonky clock
of the sun.

iv.

I need to manage my time,
so I call a meeting.
At first, I can't find time:
it ran away on me,
every time: deep time,
dark time, sweet time,
space-time, long time,
all the time.
Finally I just take time
and sit it down at the timetable
and try to get time to do a little bit more.
But "time out" is its slogan,
and in no time at all,
time has gone.

v.

Rocks: gouged by heavy-handed eons,
battered, melted, drowned, and tossed,
toasted, scraped, squished, and buried alive.
They take their time
lying down, throats cut, bones broken,
their cries too slow and stoic for us to hear.
We critters hop and pop all over them
alive and yelping,
juggling our spots and instants,
our nanos, seconds, moments,
shakes, jiffies,
ticks, ages, epochs, eras,
and even, without a second thought,
those flashes-in-the-pan,
our Stonehenges.

vi.

In the mean time, a winter gale
blows the Time Bell down.
It bangs like a bomb
in the Courtyard of Greenwich Observatory.
In no time at all,
astronomers and engineers
haul the big bell back.
Time will not get away on them.
But Hubert Airy,
son of the Astronomer Royal,
sits at his window
dreaming of sundials,
sandglasses, and water clocks
and paints a wistful watercolour
called "Time Struck Down."

vii.

Floaters in the eyes, sore knees and hips,
shoulders aching in the morning, warts and wens,
bad back, vertigo, skin cancers, acid reflux,
high blood pressure, hernia, and too damn deaf.
It's a terrible consolation,
but every day
we are becoming younger
than our dogs.

viii.

I keep a big glimmer box
in a special room
and many nights, before I go to bed,
I turn it on
so that it can vacuum
several hours out of my life.
I have shelves and shelves
of paper vacuums too.

ix.

For the time being,
here and now is indivisible.
Time beings are always
counting their papers, pounds,
and ticktocking chickens.
They number their square feet,
their sick days and their bank accounts.
Until they are well and truly dead,
they may not even see,
let alone sink into,
their fine circadian nests
of grass and light.

x.

Who makes time?
Well don't make it for me.
The dimensions are bursting at the seams.
The politician retires
to make more time for his family.
Everyone knows they don't want it.
The woman executive
wants to make time for herself.
She can cancel that yoga class right now:
there's no such thing as flow.
Each physical object
has a distinct temporal part
for every moment it exists.
You didn't have any temporal parts
before you were born.
You won't have any temporal parts
after you die.
Of course you want more.
But truly, you can't
fit any more into your life.

xi.

As I get older, I seem
to carry a cup of sadness in me
that didn't used to be there before.
When I lie down
it tips
and sadness pools
in my throat and trickles
through my ribs. Something temporal
is thawing in me.
Or it's past
its time
and has gone
bad
and is leaking.

xii.

When I hear the knell of twelve,
it seems endless.
The bell keeps chiming.
I lose count.
Was there a tune to start it off?
Did I miss the first peal?
Cinderella-ed here I am,
lost in the middle of a striking clock,
trying to stumble
out the door, failing
to match the gallop
of a child,
so unravelled, Big Banged
and finite
I know I won't
make it
to the end.

SAINT VERONICA

(who carries a veil that bears the image of Christ's face)

there is no disgusting bedsheet
the Laundress has not seen
no suspicious tear in underwear
she has not stitched
no snag from thorn or nail
she has not neatly clipped
I doubt her imagination stirred much
at this mark either

if she washed it gently at first
that is simply how laundry is done
if a rinse and some soap
won't do the job
then comes the scrub against a rock
with a handful of gravel
bleaching ash
and baking in the sun

when all else failed
she might have pawned it off
as swaddling cloth or towel
but no
clearly failing did not bother her
nor swindling

persistence is the nature
of a stain

Back when the nights
were nightier
and summers yellower,
you couldn't drive
a country mile
without getting
goop all over
your windshield.
The revolting splats—
who misses them?
But it's weird, isn't it,
all this invisible stuff
just
disappearing.

Every little corpse on the hillside
is prized by some scavenger,
vulture or squabbling crow.

But down here, we bury our pets
and burn our parents
to inedible ash.

Even the robin that hit the window
gets a shoebox funeral.
To the end, we resist
our peeps being eaten.

So it offends us when the dog,
our Zoroastrian companion,
finds two dead Bohemian waxwings
last seen at our feeder
and eats one
before we can scoop
the little corpses off the ground.

Under our noses,
the dog chomps our guest
in mouthfuls of rosy, yellow,
and nut-brown feathers.

We cradle the remaining carcass
in gloved hands,
and drop it elegantly
into a garbage can.
But it niggles.
Did we not clean
our perches weekly?

Did our birds sup
on tainted seed
from the local discount store?

Bullshit!
It was probably the cold.
Or some virus. Why are
we taking on more death?

It's true we had to kill
the mice and aphids.
And, yes, the fruit flies.
We do throw spiders and stink bugs
out the door into twenty below.
We realize the wasp trap
is pretty gruesome.

Let's not even think
about how we caught the rat,
strangled the snake
in a garden net,
and cut up ant bodies
with diatomaceous earth.

And I am sure that no one saw us
slap the dog.

BEFORE THE FLOOD

i.

I am invested in the water
that has been stockpiling all winter,
stacking avalanches into valleys,
warehousing tons of snowy freight on
mountain shelves and ramps.
Now that it's spring,
down at the creek, my Amazon,
I listen for rumours
of a colossal delivery.

ii.

How long ago was it
that looking at spring runoff
was like looking in a bank vault
or a barn filled to the rafters
or, cut the nostalgia, the Big Box store?
I barely remember building that dam.
Those were the sullen and greedy years.
I didn't know any better, or
did I?
Remember last summer?
I seem to recall
no inventory at all.
Fire, asthma, nothing you could sell.

iii.

I'm waiting for it, spending for it,
that windfall, jackpot,
free gas, groceries for life,
the big extra,
the twenty-million-dollar lottery,
even stealing from the hospice
to go to the casino.
("I couldn't have been myself.")
A big one this time
could change
the whole fucking supply chain.

thin trunks of pines and firs
thorns of black barcodes
pour out of the sky
out of shopping bags

out comes the dear downy woodpecker
soft lint from a pocket
or bird pin, red flecks
all over the floor from the dropped glass
how to deal with all that broken

could be the glass bowl
of memory, glass bowl holding the self
upside down

the hunter did return
from the woods
with knife, arrow, heart
did return and not empty-handed

holes connect everything
eyesponge of light
box mouth
ears banging their sticks in the tunnel
the tubed heart
oh door, oh key, oh screw, oh needle and thread

coal of blood sinking through snow
through the black and white woods
darkly, darkly go those footprints
barren queen
no name tags dangle
no nimble channels to change

no apples, no crown, no mirror
a white belly
some dog chewing the brains
of old ones in the home

MEAT

They say everyone eventually
gets dementia. We
flip through crosswords
and eat too much beef.
Well, they say it's dementia.
Read your *Brief Guide to Eating*. Go ahead.
Dining and driving.
Dining and driving,
is this how we have spent our lives?
Now where am I going?
Has a new wing been added
to the cafeteria?
The women
peel a strip of fat off the steak.
It's like a white belt.
You don't see that so much anymore
but I must choose my battles.
I have clung to the oven
and the steering wheel.
I have been driving and dining.
I failed to see the cows
officer, no I'm sorry, not officer.
It wasn't a road. No,
I failed the cows
be-daisied in their cagey fields.
Bessie. Bossie. Maisy. Bone.
They say, they say, what
do they say?
Why are you sticking
that shovel in my mouth?

PITTED

Is the walnut in the shell
shelled, or is the walnut
out of the shell shelled?
Is the fish gutted or
was it gutted?

The caregivers
allow me to bring cherries to my dad
but only if I pit them.
So I drill a bowlful
and feed him
one heartless
leaking
fruit
at a time.

Soon the brilliant stain
is on his face and chin,
my fingers, and within minutes
the lips of others who shuffle
into the kitchen mewing
and murmuring,
the one who thinks he's on a ship,
the one who hugs a floppy stuffy,
the one, so young, my dad
thinks is his little brother.

Ones with cheeks pitted
by absent dentures.
Ones with eyes like pits
of forgotten summer thoughts.
All gone, all there
in the feast of pitted
and once-pitted cherries.

SAINT URSULA

(after paintings of Saint Ursula by Vittore Carpaccio in Venice)

dawn, thousands of birds singing
sails, silhouetted bridges
cardinal robes parading on stinking streets
corrupted, intricate, shadowed, glistening

water, thousands of milling virgins
we: jetlagged, prone, raucously
woken early, for minutes panicked
we can't remember the plane, docking

the boat, Saint Ursula's narrow bed
a man casts a rope, a blessing
the ship tilts, a woman leans over
sleeping children aloft in masted

dreams, opening eyes and windows
the angel's gentle ascending, we unready
for the arrival of the Ambassadors, the
guidebooks open and close, arrows

strike, her funeral pyre, her virginal
fuel, we turn and toss— birds
bells, no fog dulls their clanging
in fretted vaults Madonnas croon

Bellini-brilliant, finches warbling
trees drop velvet robes of shade
carillons ornamenting the air all day
minting hallucinations with swinging

clappers, splashes, relics, drums
a massacre of girls, all those politics
it looks like a club foot, that painted limb
of the ancient Infant, deaf and dumb

IV
JULIAN

The largeness of his clothing
which were fair gathered about
means he has beclosed in him
all heavens and all joy and bliss.
—JULIAN OF NORWICH

washed, wrung, hung
out to dry
in the wind
rag that melts
when dipped
in water
rag that gloves the hand
dabs temples
and lips as
she mutters
Benedicte Domine,
is it all on fire that is here?
has smoke come wafting
through the door?
no, her burning forehead
steams
as it meets the now
transfigured cloth

he is our clothing that for love
wraps, embraces and all becloses us
not floating
above my skin
but touching shoulders, hips
clasping, unclasping
limbs oiled
with my own heat
every movement slapped
by a billow or a
collapse
the sleeve's gentle tug
at my arm, the seam's coarse
finger between my legs
the child tormented
by the shirt-tag's
wretched scrape
scrape
scrape
at the back
of his hackling neck

I took it nakedly
to my own singular person
dressed in air
each garment mere underwear
to that cold jacket
tailored with pockets and
holes
wardrobing air that lifts
my hair over collar
needleworking air that slips
a cool hand beneath
my shirt to grip
a collar bone
each pore of skin
taking the air's floss
as it moves in and
out of me, embroidered
from the moment I was
stretched over this
hoop of bones

for as the body is clothed in cloth
and the flesh in skin and the bones in flesh
and the heart in the chest, so are we
soul and body clad in the goodness of God
and enclosed
in that rare bog
that rattlin bog
embryo curled in seed
haloed in gel sac
membraned in
tomato's balloon-thin skin
all is interfretted
inwrought and corralled yet
some volcanic shoot
always bursts through—
mosquito stinger into silken sleeve
.mummy soaked in spices with
bindings all unravelling
hazelnut and hanged man dropped
needle-nose pliers drawing warp threads
through sley of the loom
organs of the body buried in heat
yet grateful for the sweater
each hair slitting the skin
on its way out—
a bloated quagmire of a stinking bog
and suddenly out of this body sprang a full fair creature
a little Child
.newborn pendent
placenta hauled
the inner doing its slippery
sliding out

we feel in us
wretches, debates and strifes
and of course lice that evolved
with our clothing
they crawl into our dearest objects
our cladding and drawers
our bed, our hair
our scarves and woolly socks
our combs and darlingest sweaters
all become warm nests
and kitchens of the louse
yet are we in all ways enclosed
till death unbuttons us
so why not
let the children run naked around the house
especially the one who cannot bear
any blistering scrap
of fabric
about his neck

on wash day
the bedding with its thousand eyes
bubbles and brims
with tears
I use that old dryer
wind and sun
so that tonight when I
lie face down in the sheets
I breathe in rinse and
prayer
all shall be well
and all manner of thing shall be well
by undressing and washing
wringing out and catching light
thirst and slake are woven into us
if we believe life is good
as in *it*
as in being alive
somewhere *it* must be well
even on this day:
the day your child
tried to hang
himself

inside a stone church
next to the priest's chasuble
embroidered with pearled
pelicans and golden stags
is the young man
nailed onto a wooden cross
he was hanging up in the air
as men hang a cloth to dry
she locked herself up
and saw all the world
in the seed of a tree
I sit in her cell
weeping and breaking
every stick of so-called strength
in my heart
my poor boy, my poor boy
two hours with my eyes
flooding, oozing
above me blood
dangling from ribs and splinters
pooling on
that blindfold around
the young man's hips

a double thirst
both bodily and ghostly
washing machine and dryer
a carpet cleaner van
with soapy tank, mighty vacuum
and yards of hose
two kinds of secrets
four kinds of dread
three ways of beholding
when rugs, quilts, cloaks
all manner of heavy fabrics
needed cleaning
they were thumped
and beaten
three things that belong to our prayers
two workings
seven great pains
two kinds of sickness
the Norwich Museum has the best
collection of truncheons
in the country

I it am
every day getting dressed
and undressed
or maybe never changing at all
like the child
like the anchoress in her cell
I it am
is the mantra of folding and unfolding
the *it* pleated into
the middle of our being
skirt bunched in hand
to wash in the tub
or hurry down the street
I it am
grammar breaking us open
grammar pushing the candy in the middle
priests circle *it* for centuries
keep asking: is *it* nakedness or clothing
which sings of sight over
darkness, beauty over
bliss?

the sweet skin and tender flesh
with the hair and the blood loosed above from the bone
with the thorns where it was dagged in many pieces
as a cloth that was sagging
she must have trussed many a chicken
roasted the meat till
falling off the bone
marvelled at how cooked blood
silkens into gravy
our precious Mother Jesus
he may feed us with himself
a holiday, a feast
crumbs fall from the table
dogs lick the floor, the tablecloth is stained
but friends and family are full
of thanksgiving, cracking
backbone and ribs
making soup with the remains
everyone talking and laughing but the son
outside the kitchen window
in the dark, smoking
a cigarette, the glass clouding over
I warm my hands
in the soapy glove of dishwater
but the tea towel
is sopping and useless
how tools shift in our hands
the skewer wears a collar of crusty fat
hazelnut in the stuffing
forks into a tree

thrash that tablecloth
scatter the crumbs
on the snow for the birds
all certainties
shall be shaken in sorrow and anguish and tribulation
in this world,
as men shake a cloth in the wind
throw out the cheese with the chaff
the shabby, the righteous, the bullies
the liars, the lonely, the sweethearts
in as much as we fail, in so much we fall
and in as much as we fall
in so much we die
for we must die
there will be no winnowing here
every holy and unholy fleck will fly
after the feast, the fall
after it's beaten senseless, the winter
the cleansing's but a walloping
in the wind

she tells us to practise the art
of letting things happen
the shrub excretes berries
the body of the bear opens and shuts
in the forest's felt hands
bear scat is served on plate of leaf
which beetles eat from underneath
she tells us to appreciate the steady stream
of *enjoying, mourning, desire, dread and the secure true hope*
running right through us
turn the earth upside down,
and seek the deepness
don't be repelled by
the fungus-fingered
groping of the world
the spindling bowels that
ply shit
into the steaming rope
that makes
the mighty mantle
of the earth

driving down the street
I glimpse someone shuffling
head down
through rain and desolation
my heart alarms
is it my child? no
it's another
another human being
whatever you do, you will have sorrow
inside your heart
you will find at least one
of the four failures of love:
neglect, denial, contempt, and cruelty
I am driving
my hands are clenched
my knees bent
I have been angry and afraid
miserable and deluded
our failing is dreadful,
our falling is shameful
a man bundled against the wind
crosses a barren field
I drive away
in all this the sweet eye of pity and love
never leaves us
always now
that wretched scratch, scratch, scratch
at the back of the neck

behold the hazelnut tree
its ornate and filthy sandals
its brown eyes
a hazelnut in the palm of my hand
leafy dress billowing open, pleating
and dropping
in the wind
"What may this be?"
more than sacred grove
more than a thousand branches woven
with loom of root and air
a single glossy hazelnut
"All that is made"
inside it inside

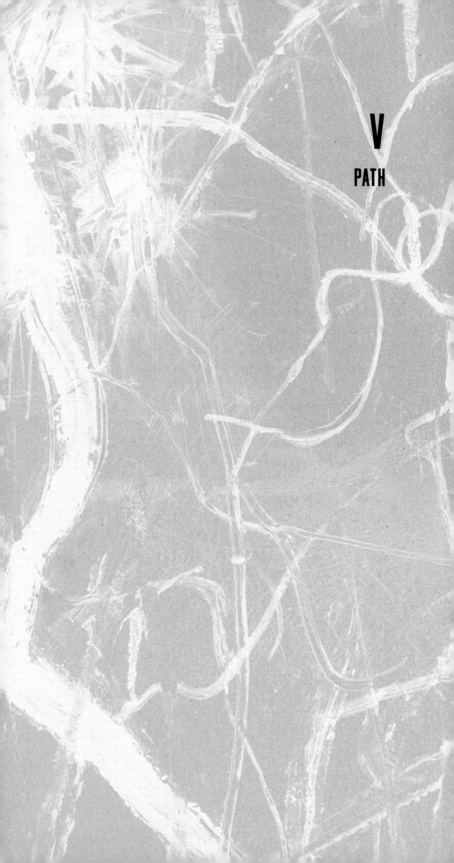

V

PATH

SAINT CAINNECH

(patron saint of the shipwrecked)

A foot of snow has fallen overnight.
I strap on snowshoes and begin to pad uphill
to take a sunrise walk. Some earlier pilgrim
has come this way and in their poking steps
I neatly tamp a frozen channel and smooth
the path for other travellers when they come.

I plod in cold and steady thought until
I reach a shocking slash right through my course.
A deer's plunging heart-shaped hooves have wrecked
my tidy, narrow route, torpedoed my line
into a frothy, wayward X. Spun round,
unmoored like when the saint's living lectern,

a spellbound stag, bolted in fear, all study
scattered, the Good Book bouncing in its rack.
Still, saint, stag and Book were soon restored.
But there's no salvage here. The snow tells
of feet sinking, paths crossed, heart churned,
and all devotion to order overturned.

A way is both a method and direction,
clear instructions and a map for going,
how to love and be, or where to run,
a poem that's both a baffling and a showing.

after a long night out
after the wine and the gin
after I heard someone say she trashed her car after closing time
when I was drunk and tired
hours in stifling sheets
cursing the uselessness of 3 a.m.
after caffeine, after reading novels in one sitting
and stepping on the dog in the dark
after seeing the moon just get up and leave
after the crying and worry
that is eating me alive
after the paralysis and procrastination
after I tried to watch TV but don't know how to use
                the three remotes
after ruining the settings on the TV
after buying LED bulbs because the lights were on all night
feeling guilty about the waste, about my mother, about
                the child
after the snapping impatience
being sick on bad chocolate, herbal tea and Facebook
after watching the windows cut up the moon
into little squares before it ditched us
after I sat on the couch in a blanket
after the owl hooted for an hour in a clacking tree
after thinking how the body's organs
work just fine in the dark
then thinking that's some stupid consolation
after I wanted to do more and I wanted to do less
after my lover fell asleep
after clenching my jaw, after wearing dental appliances
after pills and hot baths
after feeling my emptiness
and acknowledging it maturely

after renunciation and peace and meditation
failed
after I didn't even want any
so there, so I broke down
I gave up the alarm
I gave up the rest
I said I'd sleep in and they can get up and do it all
like the selfish bitch that I am
then I came back to the morning
the *morning*
my friend

THE WAY WE ARE MADE OF

in the fall
milkweed seeds parachute
into the unknown
a fleet of giddy exiles

they camp on fiery compost
drop their frying pans in flames
and wait till frost cracks
their brûlée

soon all that remains
is mashed fur and feathers
though the world still wears
their empty hangars

and decaying mansions
relics of summer's melodrama
when Monarchs lost
the crown of wild bees

ball gowns blazed into muskets
firecrackers bloomed
and treasure was feverishly
socked away in caskets

in their boudoirs, the seeds
heard caterpillars tunnelling
so it was now or never: jailed for life
or break away, leave the silken nest

for a new life stripped down
to the Nothing that is Everything
in the holy filth and covenant
of soil

PATHS TAKEN

i.

Paths in their courtesy and tricks.
Paths through the sound of water.
Paths that have the hots for lungs and knees.
Paths through the grass's dusty thoughts.
Paths being born.
Paths leaving well enough behind.
Paths where your footprints lie on top of others.
Paths where your feet are bathed in blue light.
Paths full of tresses and passes.
Paths slipping down the back of an otter.
Paths that are the Way
and the way out.

ii.

I am thinking of myself as I was
at the bottom of this path.
I had not gone anywhere yet.
My eyes were blank where soon
there would be wildflowers.
I had not seen bluebirds nor had a snake
slither between my feet.
I had not been stung by nettles nor by cactus.
I had not sat in a meadow of perfumed grass
and leaned upon a death camas.
I had not heard my footsteps on crunchy moss
nor found old bitterroot blooms
pale as porcelain teacups
in the pine needles.
Oh I was a hapless creature
future-blind, present-poor,
and past-pulled.

iii.

The forest paths wander
in and out of their directions.
Animals contour and sculpt
the hillside with their secret lives.
Their feet unearth flavours and layers,
a bed drops down here,
dung rolls down there.
A reckless Christmas string of ice
treks along
the cliffside.
The traipsing
of the pine's branches
sweeps away the prints of deer and squirrel
and erases
the quail's hieroglyphic dance
in snow.

NOTES

"Arborophobia," sometimes spelled "Arboraphobia," means fear and hatred of trees. It was likely coined by architect Robin Boyd in his 1960 book *The Australian Ugliness*. The term describes the tendency of architects, developers, landscapers, agriculturalists, and Western society in general to transform ecosystems by destroying trees and native plants, ostensibly in the name of aesthetics and culture.

Milk chutes were a peculiar and now obsolete feature of houses on the Canadian prairies when I was growing up. The milk chute was a cupboard built into the wall of the house to be used by that other obsolescence, the milkman. The chute had an exterior door that the milkman could open to deposit the milk bottles, and an interior door for those inside the house to retrieve the fresh bottles and place the empties for return.

The epigraph for "Anemone in Cyprus" is from Horst Weierstall, *From Sign to Action: Drawings, Drafts, Traces* (Moufflon, 2004).

The stories of the saints are wild and numerous. Saint Lucy was a Christian martyr in the early fourth century who reputedly had her eyes gouged out when she was executed. Saint Veronica was said to have wiped the face of Christ as he was carrying the Cross and his face became imprinted on the cloth she used. The horrific legend of Saint Ursula involves her leading 11,000 virgins on a pilgrimage; on the way back home they all were slaughtered when Ursula refused to marry a pagan chief. Her story is told in a series of paintings by Vittore Carpaccio that can be seen at the Accademia Galleries in Venice. Saint Cainnech (the Irish name of Saint Kenneth) was a sixth century abbot and missionary in Ireland and Scotland. There are many fabulous stories about him, including his reading the Bible as it rested in the antlers of a stag, and his saving his friend Columba from shipwreck through telepathic means.

In the sequence "A Cloth in the Wind, or Being with Julian of Norwich," italicized words are by Julian of Norwich, taken from *Showing of Love*, translated by Julia Bolton Holloway (Darton, Longman and Todd/The Liturgical Press, 2003). The epigraph for the collection, and for the section "Julian," are from the same volume. Julian of Norwich was an English anchoress and mystic who lived in the medieval textile town of Norwich, when Europe was reeling from the catastrophic pandemic of the Black Plague. Her book of theology, *Showing of Love*, is the earliest surviving English-language book written by a woman. Julian's anchorage—or cell—was housed in the Saint Julian parish church in Norwich. Mother Julian, or Dame Julian, took the name of the church when she became an anchoress. She was essentially a recluse who lived in the church and spent her life in prayer and devotions. The church was destroyed in World War II. It has been rebuilt with a quiet chapel for meditation where Julian's cell might have been.

The epigraph for "The Time Being" is from Aristotle, *Physics*, Book 4, part 13. Translated by R.P. Hardie and R.K. Gaye, http://classics.mit.edu/Aristotle/physics.4.iv.html.

ACKNOWLEDGEMENTS

The following poems were written with dedications: "Anemone in Cyprus" to Arianna Economou; "Newborn" to Toby Hoyte; "Early Spring Elegy" in memory of Sylvia Russell; "How I Came Back to the Morning" to Karen Connelly.

Some of these poems, or versions of them, have been previously published as follows:

"Dementia, the Queen" in *Arc Poetry Magazine*, Summer 2014. Winner of Editors' Choice Poem of the Year contest.

"Meat and Dementia" in *Memory and Loss: A Canadian Anthology of Poetry to support the Alzheimer Society of Ontario*, edited by I.B. Iskov (Ink Bottle Press, 2016).

"Paths Taken" in *FreeFall* 27.1 (Spring 2017).

"The Tribes of Grass" in *Crannóg* 47 (Spring 2018).

"Pitted" in *The New Quarterly*, Winter 2018.

"Ponderosa Pine" in *Heartwood: Poems for the Love of Trees*, edited by Lesley Strutt (League of Canadian Poets, 2018).

"Anemone in Cyprus" in *Eco Art Incubator Cyprus: Sites Embodied*, edited by Nancy Holmes and Denise Kenney (Lake Publishing, 2019).

"The Way We Are Made Of" was first published as a video poem at the FarmFolk CityFolk Seedy Saturday online conference, February 22, 2021 (https://youtube/XI6xj1fepqU).

"Saint Cainnech" in *Literary Review of Canada*, March 2022.

The sequence "Ponderosa Pine" was inspired by the ponderosa pine paintings of Teresa Posyniak, and versions of some poems were exhibited with her work at the Christine Klassen Gallery in Calgary and published in a chapbook about the paintings: *Ponderosa: Paintings by Teresa Posyniak and Poems by Nancy Holmes* (Abbisibbia Press, 2019).

I am deeply grateful to the Ontario Heritage Trust for a month of writing and reading at the Doris McCarthy Artist-in-Residence Centre at Fool's Paradise. Within that serene and artist-centered space, I began studying Julian of Norwich and writing the poems that eventually became "A Cloth in the Wind."

Thanks to Karen Connelly and Sharon Thesen for reading early versions or parts of this manuscript and providing encouragement and advice. I am full of gratitude for the insight and generosity of Sharon Thesen, who edited these poems. I am also grateful to the anonymous peer reviewers of the University of Alberta Press for their insightful reading and comments.

Love and gratitude to Dave, as always.

Other Titles from University of Alberta Press

SEPARATION ANXIETY

GAVIN BRADLEY

This poignant debut explores the emotional toll of different kinds of separation: from a partner, a previously held sense of self, or a home and the people left behind. *Separation Anxiety* ultimately conveys a message of hope, reminding us that "we'll be remembered for / ourselves, and not the spaces we / leave behind."

Robert Kroetsch Series

WELCOME TO THE ANTHROPOCENE

ALICE MAJOR

Alice Major observes the comedy and the tragedy of this human-dominated moment on Earth. Major's most persistent question—"Where do we fit in the universe?"—is made more urgent by the ecological calamity of human-driven climate change. Her poetry leads us to question human hierarchies, loyalties, and consciousness, and challenges us to find some humility in our overblown sense of our cosmic significance.

Robert Kroetsch Series

RAIN SHADOW

NICHOLAS BRADLEY

Rain Shadow is a collection of poetry that explores the fraught relationship between the natural world and humans yearning to connect with something greater than themselves. Witty, playful, serious, and heartsore, *Rain Shadow* seeks to understand the space in which people and nature are inextricably entwined.

Robert Kroetsch Series

More information at uap.ualberta.ca